ANIMALS, ANIMALS, ANIMALS
Book Series Number One
Starring
PELICANS, CATS and FROGS
From The Award Winning ABC Television Children's Series:
A Creation of ABC News

Written by Lester Cooper
Executive Producer and Director and Writer of the
ANIMALS, ANIMALS, ANIMALS, Television Series

Edited by Julie Duffy

Illustrated by Ed Cage and Novle Rogers

Photography by H. Michael Stewart

1

For Audrey, who raised our animals from the beginning and somehow turned them into people.

We wish to gratefully acknowledge the American Broadcasting Company and The News Operation for their complete cooperation. Also we wish to thank the staff of ANIMALS, ANIMALS, ANIMALS, for their help and enthusiasm.

EDITOR

Written by Lester Cooper and hosted by Hal Linden, ABC's ANIMALS, ANIMALS, ANIMALS has received the following awards:

The distinguished *Peabody Award* for excellence in children's TV programming. (The Peabody Award is one of the most prestigious and coveted awards in TV).

The Action For Children's Television Award (celebrating an achievement in children's television).

Endorsed by *The National Educational Association* which represents over 1,800,000 teachers across the country.

ANIMALS, ANIMALS, ANIMALS — Series 1
Starring Pelicans, Cats and Frogs
First Edition Published 1978
Copyright © 1978 by Handel and Sons, Publishing, Inc.
All rights reserved, including the right to
reproduce this book or any parts thereof.
ISBN 0-917080-03-3
Library of Congress Catalog Card Number 78-050972

Handel and Sons, Publishing, Inc.
14001 Goldmark, Suite 242
Dallas, Texas 75204

Foreword
by Roger Caras

If you want to do something good in this world (or something well) the first thing you must do is care. ANIMALS, ANIMALS, ANIMALS is a good television show that has been well done because a man called Lester Cooper cares.

The show and the book are clearly the work of a man who feels the importance of what he is doing. That is perhaps why the show has won just about every award it is eligible for.

Our lives are intertwined with all of the other creatures that are sailing through time on our spaceship, Earth, with us. As far back as the records of man go, we have been involved with animals, subject to the same rules of life and living. In ANIMALS, ANIMALS, ANIMALS, Lester Cooper explores that interest and examines the rules of life and living.

One thing is certain, no one but Lester Cooper could have done it, not and have had it come out with the same warm sense of both sense and nonsense. In a way, I guess you could say, Lester Cooper is the father of ANIMALS, ANIMALS, ANIMALS. What a lovely family he has created.

Pelicans

Pelicans

A Pelican *isn't* man's best friend
But he's a *friendly* kind of Bird.

Though you really *must admit*,
That he sometimes looks **ABSURD!**

These are pelicans . . . .

Which is *no surprise* to the Pelicans
You are *not* a Pelican, which is *certainly* no surprise
to the Pelicans.
But if you've never *seen* a Pelican, a Pelican can be
very surprising.
Especially out of water.
We're going to meet some Pelicans in the water,
and out of it.
If *you're* not surprised . . . . . *I'll* be surprised!

8

THE PELICAN IS A VERY FUNNY BIRD.

The Pelican is
not *funny, funny* . . . .
Just **FUNNY**.
For instance,
most Pelicans nest on the ground.
Pelicans only eat fish.
Pelicans have only four toes.
Of course,
they have webbed feet.
In this edition of ANIMALS, ANIMALS, ANIMALS,
we are going to meet the Pelican.
In *fact,*
we are going to meet *lots* of Pelicans.

Now a Pelican is *here* . . . .

New Zealand

Australia

and a Pelican is *there* . . . .

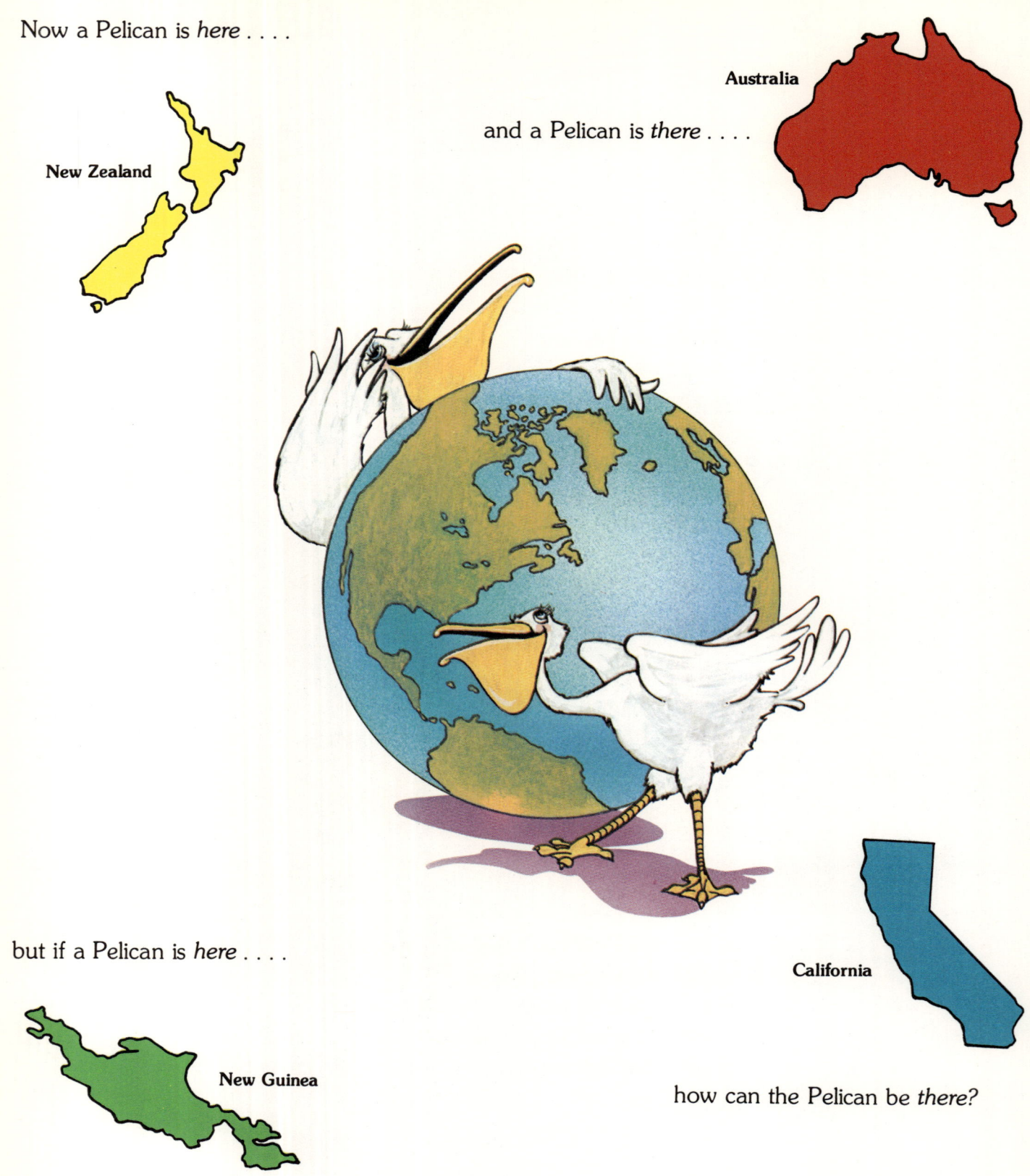

but if a Pelican is *here* . . . .

California

New Guinea

how can the Pelican be *there*?

This may seem like a silly question,
but to put it another way . . . .
where oh *where* is the Pelican?

Where oh where is the Pelican?

There are Pelicans in the *water*,
And Pelicans in the *air*.
And once you could find Pelicans
Almost *everywhere*.

There are Pelicans on islands in
New Zealand and Australia.
The Pelican is a kind of a Bird that
Very *seldom* fails ya.

The Pelican is a web-footed Bird
That's much *larger* than a Duck.
And you can see them in New Guinea
With a little *luck*.

The Pelican comes in brown and white
In *fact, he changes* color
And Pelicans can *still* be found along
The coast of California.

There are Pelicans in Nevada, and on
Utah's Great Salt Lake,
And in spite of the fact that the
Pelican's gone, Louisiana's still
Called the *Pelican State*.

If you've ever seen a Pelican fish
Then no doubt you've seen his pouch.
And you've got to *admit* when it comes
To the Fish, the Pelican's *no slouch*.

So now we know where the Pelican
Is and where he can be found.
But we'd better start taking *care* of him
If we want to keep him around.

There are Pelicans in the water,
And Pelicans in the air.
And once you could find Pelicans
Almost everywhere.

It would be nice if the Pelican
Still, was almost everywhere.

The Pelican Can

The Pelican can, the Pelican can
Catch a fish in his *pouch* he can.

A Pelican is a web-footed bird
And the strange thing about him,
He is *seldom heard*.

In fact, a Pelican has *no voice*.
Though he *does* make some sound to
The *girl* of his choice.

Well, the Pelican is one bird that does not sing.
But how nice it is to sing a song *about the Pelican*.
So here's a song to sing.... about the PELICAN, *of course!*

If Only I Had a Pelican's Pouch

If only I had a Pelican's pouch
The *things* that I could *do,*
Fill it with rings and wonderful things
And give them all to you, to you,
Fill it with *rings* and *wonderful things*
And give them *all to you.*

If only I had a Pelican's pouch
The things that I could do
Pack it with *gold* and *riches untold*
And I'd give them *all* to you.
Pack it with *gold* and *riches untold*
And I'd give them *all to you,* to you.

If only I had a Pelican's pouch
The things that I could *do,*
Fill it with *kisses* and *candies delicious*
And give them all to you, to you.
Fill it with *kisses* and *candies delicious*
And give them *all to you.*

If only I had a Pelican's pouch
The *things* that I could *do,*
Pack it with *dresses* and *other things precious*
And wear them *all for you.*

So whenever you see something *funny*
On a beast or bird or man,
Think what it *might* do,
Something that you
Can't do
And wished you *can* . . . .

Something that you
Can't do
And wished you *can!*

Thomas Wolf & Michael Kamen © Copyright 1976
American Broadcasting Music, Inc., ABC/Dunhill
Music Inc. Used by permission—all rights reserved.

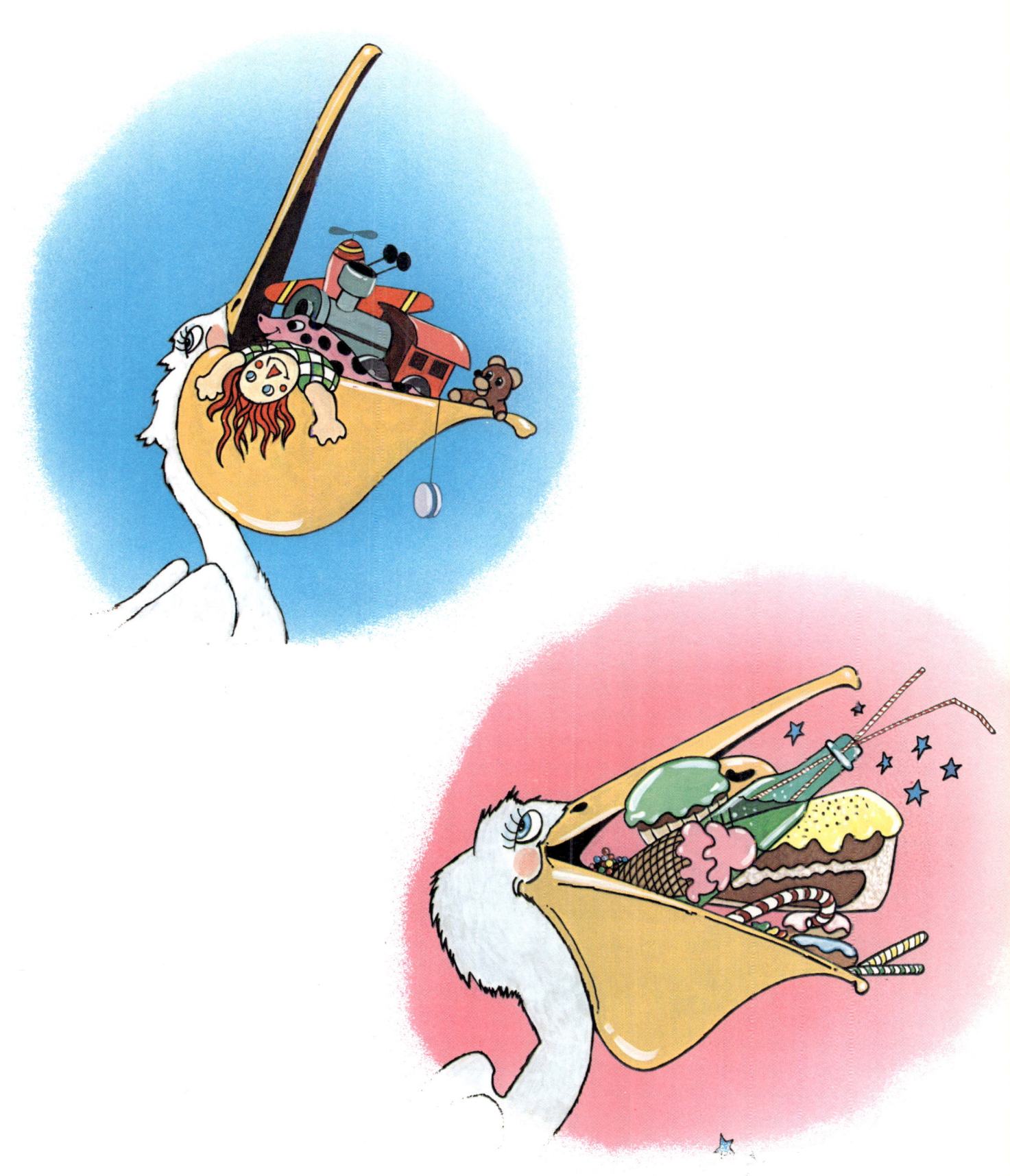

The Pelican

A PRETTY RIDICULOUS BIRD

Now, there are some people who still believe the
Pelican is a *pretty ridiculous bird*.
You've got to admit, the Pelican is not *exactly*
what you would call *gainly,* which is, of course,
the opposite of *ungainly,* which, according to the
dictionary means: not graceful, awkward, clumsy,
and uncouth.
And *that* is certainly a terrible thing to say about
any bird . . . . don't you agree?
For myself, I would not say *that* about my best friend,
would you?
Even though my best friend is *certainly* one smart bird.
However, he is certainly *not* a Pelican. In spite of
the fact that he is *extremely* sociable.
But to get back to the Pelican,
which is also an extremely sociable bird, it is true,
that a Pelican on the ground does not move *exactly* like
a *ballet dancer!*

In *fact*, it could be said that if there had not been any Swans around, and only Pelicans, when Tchaikovsky wrote the ballet *Swan Lake*, it is highly unlikely that he would have written . . . *Pelican Lake* . . . though there are three lakes called *Pelican Lake* in the state of Minnesota and one in the state of Wisconsin . . . .
However, they were not named by Tchaikovsky.

A WINNER.........................

Who can say that the Pelican in full color is not a *beautiful* bird?

Obviously, only someone who has *never seen* a Pelican in full color.

Start with the chicks.

Which in Pelican talk, means *baby.* Poor things, They're *naked,* but watch!

First, the white down begins to cover them . . . .
soon some brown feathers on the back and the head . . . .
then the neck with white feathers on the down side . . . .
see how they grow!

The back and wing feathers turn silver.

And the white feathers become black.

The head and the neck turn to white.

.......WITH FLYING COLORS

The colors change with the seasons.
There are winter and early spring colors:
yellow.
white.
black.
pink.
and shades of orange.

A running start into the wind, like an airplane,
and away . . . . **they fly.**
Ridiculous bird?
Beautiful Pelican.
. . . . **a winner**
. . . . *with flying colors*

19

KEEP THE PELICAN FLYING ON

The Pelican is surprising
In so very many ways,
And likes to fish in the water,
Which is where he spends his days.

He herds the fish and scoops them up
Into his great big pouch
Which may seem *strange*
To the fish in the water,
But the Pelican is no *slouch*.

He raises his bill and drains the water,
And then, raises his head for his dinner,
And before a fish knows what's going on
Why the Pelican's got the fish inner!

The Pelican *dives* and also *swims*
And even *sleeps* in the water.
But the Pelican's feathers always stay dry
The mother, the father, the *daughter*.

It's sad to say that this bird today
Is becoming rarer and rarer.
And the browns are on the *endangered* list
It's time *we decided* to spare her,

From disappearing from the waters and skies
For when she's *gone*, she's *gone*.
So let's do our best to unpollute
And keep **the Pelican flying on!**

The Pelican

It's *absurd*!!! It's *funny*!!! It's *ridiculous*!!!
It's **the Pelican.**
And now that you have *met* the Pelican,
Are you surprised?
If *you're* not surprised . . . .
Then . . . . *I'm* surprised.

So let me repeat . . .
There are Pelicans in the *water,* and
Pelicans in the *air.*
And once you could find Pelicans
Almost *everywhere.*
It would be nice if the Pelican *still,*
Was almost *everywhere.*

Now we know where the Pelican *is*
And where he can be *found.*
But we'd better *start caring* for him
If we want to keep him around.

at

Now there's no *question* that a Cat
Usually knows where it's *at*

And can a **Cat,**
Or *anyone* for that matter
Ask for *anything more?*

The Cat's Meow

In this edition of ANIMALS, ANIMALS, ANIMALS, we're going to find out all about the Cat, or *at least,* as much as the *Cat* will let us know.

The Cat has paws and claws, and if you've ever heard of the *Cat's Meow,* that's just what a *lot* of people *think* of the Cat.

There are about 30 million house Cats in the United States.

The average Cat is eight to ten inches tall. That's the average, full grown house Cat, of course.

It lives about fifteen years, and in spite of the fact that the Cat *has whiskers,* the Cat does not *shave.* . . .

A Cat is a pet. If you *pet* your pet, is the pet that you *pet* necessarily a *Cat*? *Not necessarily*. But who *wouldn't* want a Cat for a pet? To *pet*?

Now *this* is a *Cat!*

It's not just *any* old Cat.
It is not a Siamese or a Persian or a Tabby Cat . . . . . This is a Panthera Leo better known as a *Lion*.

But it is *important* to remember that a *Lion* is not a House Cat and should under no circumstances be considered a pet to *pet*.

It's Really Great to be a Cat

It's really *great* to be a Cat
And always know just where you're at.

To climb a tree or sit and stare,
A Cat can go *almost anywhere*.

A Cat can play with a ball of string.
A Cat has a *ball* with almost any old thing.

And while it's true that a *Cat* can *scratch*,
It's a well-known fact he can also *catch*

A Mouse or a Bird or even a *Rat*.
Is there a person alive who can do all *that*?

And while a Cat is *extremely inscrutable*,
You'll seldom see any one thing more beautiful!

It walks with *elegance* on the tips of its toes
The Cat has *great dignity* wherever it goes.

It can arch its back and look twice its size
Sit by the hour without blinking its *eyes*.

It can curl itself into a ball
It can twitch its tail and *that's* not all.

It can keep you warm when it climbs in
Your lap.

Stretch out by the fire and take a *catnap*.
A Cat is a *wonderful, wonderful* pet.

That drinks milk from a saucer with *such
Etiquette*.

A Cat is so nice to have in the house.
Unless, *of course*, it's the house of a *Mouse*.

Now of *course*, no self respecting Mouse
would invite a *Cat* into his house, or for
that matter - a *Lion*,
which we *know* is a Cat.

There is a fable about *belling* the Cat.
It has *absolutely nothing* to do with a Lion,
although the Lion is *certainly* a member of the
Cat family. I mean, look at it this way,
not just *anybody* can bell the Cat.
Imagine trying to bell a Lion, which is also a *Cat*.

The leopard is a member of the cat family.

FABLE

Belling the Cat

A very, very long time ago, which was a very long time before now and longer ago than just very long ago, the Mice world decided to have a General Council to consider what measure they could take to outwit their common enemy . . . . the Cat.

The meeting was called to order: "The meeting is called to order," said the Mouse Chief. Immediately, one of the Mice stood up. "I believe," she said, "that we should build a better Cat trap."

All of the Mice at the General Council laughed. "A better Cat trap!" the Mouse Chief said in astonishment.

FABLE

"There is no such thing as a Cat trap at *all* so how, pray tell, can we build a better one?" And that was the end of *that* suggestion.

Now a very young Mouse stood up. "I have," he said, "a proposal to make which I think will meet the case."
"*Speak,* young Mouse," said the Mouse Chief.
"Notice," said the young Mouse, "the *sly* and *treacherous* manner in which our enemy approaches us. You will all agree," he went on, "if we could receive some *signal* of the Cat's approach, we could easily escape from the Cat."

He looked around the Council for approval and waited for a moment.

FABLE

Finally, he said: "I venture, therefore, to propose that a small bell be procured and attached by a ribbon around the neck of the Cat."

Now there was *much applause* by the Council and they all smiled at the young Mouse. Then, when the applause died down, a very old and dignified Mouse got up. "That is all very well," he said very slowly in a very wise voice, "but who is to bell the Cat?" *Nobody spoke.*

FABLE

"It is *easy*," he said, "to propose *impossible remedies*. But it is well to remember to look at both sides of a question if you want to find the solution."
"You are *right*," Said the Chief Mouse. "And I now adjourn the meeting so that we can better *examine* the *question*."

So all of the Mice went back to their holes and the belling of the cat was left to the girls and boys and ladies and gentlemen. *However*, it is important to *remember* that the belling of the Cat is *strictly for the birds*.

Now as everyone knows, *Cats love Birds.* But *Birds,* though they can *sing,* certainly do not want to sing for the Cat's supper.
Now *here* are a lot of different kinds of *Cats* you can *sing* about:

Cat Song

Curiosity killed the Cat.
We *all* know that.
But I got curious just the same
And tried to see if I could name
The major breeds of Cat I swear
They're just two groups: long and short hair.
And they include:
Siamese Cats and Burmese Cats
The Persian and Abyssinian.
When you've said *that,* you're just *beginnin'* em.
The Himalayan and the Paraguayan;
Angora, Rex and Russian Blue;
And the Japanese Kimono, too.
Don't forget the Tibetan Temple,
The Lop-Eared Breed, whose *ears* are *ample.*
Oriental Bobtail and Malay
And that leaves just *one* more to say:
Manx. You're welcome.
Now see if *you* can repeat them all.

Thomas Wolf & Lynn Kellogg © Copyright 1976 American Broadcasting Music, Inc. Used by permission—all rights reserved.

Manx

Black Persian

American Short Hair

Odd-Eyed Persian

Rex

Abyssinian

SIMPLY PUR-R-R-R-R-R-RFECT

There are Black Cats, Brown Cats, House Cats, Wild Cats, and of course, other Cats *that,* by any other name are *still Cats,*
as we know . . . .
However, it is important to remember, that a *Cat* which *is* a Cat, no matter what it is called, is *without question,*
a *Cat.*
Which is probably why *Cats* resemble *other Cats.*
All Cats, for instance, have large eyes.
They have ears they can turn sideways, which makes it possible for them to listen in all directions.
They have long, stout whiskers that keep them from running into things at night, and possibly injuring their eyes.
And of course, as we know, a Cat . . . . is . . . . a . . . Cat. Just that!
One more thing: Cats **pur-r-r-r-r.** Which may just be why Cats are simply **pur-r-r-r-rfect**
Don't you *agree?*

Himalayan

Siamese

Berman

In *fact* you might even call the House Cat a *Hip* Cat.
I have something to say about the House Cat that
should make *any* Cat sit up and take notice.

A HIP CAT

There are Cats that live inside a house
And even call it home.
And you'll find them in the Coliseum whenever
You're in Rome.

There are Tabby Cats and Tortoiseshells
And Cats that come from Burma.
A Cat can jump from the highest tree and land
On Terra Firma.

A Cat is good at catching Mice and some
Are known as Mousers.
But very few if any Cats are ever seen
In trousers.

A Cat can walk and run and play and you can
Hear a Cat's meow.
Could we have done without the Cat, ...
I can't imagine how.

Hey Cat, ... are you a **hip cat?**

IT'S ALL ....

There are Cat lovers,
and Cat haters which
may be hard to believe.
The Egyptians called the Cat
the Goddess of Moonlight, Fertility,
Wisdom, and Hunting back in 2600 B.C.
In 525 B.C. the Persians fought the
Egyptians; they carried cats into battle, and the
Egyptians retreated.

Julius Caesar, Emperor of Rome, was a cat hater.
The ancient Chinese were Cat lovers. They believed
the Cat brought *good luck*.

In Japan, the Cat was welcomed in the Royal Palace because
it protected the Silkworms from Rodents. The Japanese
placed statues of Cats at doorways believing they would
scare away *Rats* and *evil*. They were Cat lovers.

In the first century B.C., the Romans invaded the
British Isles, and they brought the Cat with them.
The Roman Cat mated with the British Wild Cat and the Wild
Cat was domesticated . . . . . . laws were passed to protect
the Cat, and the Cat protected the people from Rats.
At that time most people were Cat lovers.

40

HISTORY

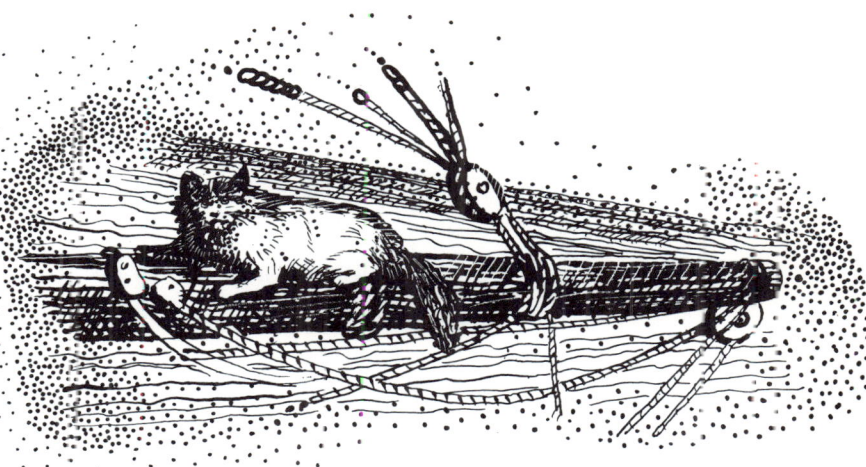

But then in the Middle Ages, many people believed the Cat was a *witch* . . . *agent of the devil* . . . . they burned them, drowned them but when the ships of the Crusaders brought the Black Cat to the low Countries and Britain, they also carried *Rats*. The Rats brought the *plague,* which was a great sickness and the people were saved when the Cat brought the Rats under control. And the people once more became Cat lovers.

During the Renaissance, which followed the Middle Ages in Europe, the Cat could be found in Art. The Cat is in Pietro Lorenzetti's painting, *The Last Supper.* Many artists were Cat lovers. Under Louis the Fifteenth Cats were given the freedom of the city of Paris to please the queen, who was a Cat lover.

The emperor, Napoleon, was a Cat hater. The Colonists brought the Cat to America. They took the Cat to church to keep themselves warm. They were Cat lovers. Many well-known writers were Cat lovers. Charles Dickens was a Cat lover, so was Rudyard Kipling. Henry James wrote with a Cat on his shoulder. Mark Twain was a Cat lover; so was Samuel Johnson, Ernest Hemingway, and Walt Whitman, who in fact resembled a Cat . . . . Cat lovers all!

And of *course,* there is Mehitable who believed she was once Cleopatra, which certainly brings us right back to where the Cat was first loved . . . . . *Egypt.*

Could we have done without the cat?

People and Cats have been together for a
long time.
The Cat came into man's life really on its
own about 10,000 years ago.
It was not man's choice or desire to
domesticate the Cat . . . . the *Cat* made that
decision.

Astonishingly enough, some people do *not like* Cats.
Although I can't imagine *who* would not like Cats.
Now we are going to meet some Cat Lovers and some
Cat Haters.
If you're not *amazed* by *who* is *which*,
I'll be amazed.

NOBODY REALLY OWNS THE CAT!

There are Cats that roam in alleys
While others live in style.
And while a Cat has *whiskers,*
It is hard to see her *smile.*

You can see them in a Cat show,
With sleek and shining fur.
You can pet them when they *are* your pet
And sometimes make them **pur-r-r-r.**

A Lion's just a great, big, Cat,
And a Leopard shows its spots.
A baby Cat's a *Kitten*
That gets cuddled *lots* and *lots.*

There are long hair Cats and short
Haired Cats and *some* are Siamese.
But there's very little question,
A Cat is very hard to *please.*

Yes, a Cat is very nice to have around
In *fact,* a Cat's a *pleasure.*
But nobody really owns a Cat, it's the *Cat*
That takes . . . . . *your* measure.

Now we've seen the Cat being what the Cat is . . .
a **Cat.**
Something very special about the Cat:
it has *independence,*
it has *dignity.*
It is *exactly* what it is.
Nothing more.
Nothing less.
Who can ask any more from an animal . . . .
or a *person* . . . . for that matter?

Now let's take a giant step or maybe a *jump,* with
the *Frog* and the *Toad.*
We know cats *meow.*
And Pelicans *fish.* They also, of course, *fly.*
As for *Frogs* and *Toads* . . . . . you may just find out more
than you ever thought there was to know about the
Frog and the Toad. Or the other way around, if you
like.
As everyone knows, there are *Frogs* and there are *Toads.*
You didn't?
You will when you turn the page . . . .
Oh, yes.
There are also *Tadpoles* which grow up to be *Toads*
or *Frogs.*
Or, of course, *vice versa.*

Animals, Animals, Animals Continues With Toads and Frogs

FROG

The Best of Both Worlds

In case you didn't know, a Frog is an *Amphibian,* which means that it lives on land and in water, which *certainly* gives it the best of *both* worlds.

But did you know that an Amphibian, which is what a Frog is, never drinks the *water*? How about *that*?

Now that you know *that,* you might find what you are about to see and read about the Frog *absolutely fascinating*.

It has long, hind legs, which allows it to make those long jumps. It has large, bulging eyes, which can *see* in almost every direction which makes it pretty hard to creep up on a Frog . . . . *even* from behind.

In this edition of ANIMALS, ANIMALS, ANIMALS we're going to meet a lot of Frogs and they may just make *your* eyes bulge!

Texas Toad

Great Plains Toad

Frogs and Toads

Sonoran Green Toad

Spadefoot Frog

A Tadpole, which is *sometimes* called a Polliwog, is *not* a Frog or a Toad. But there is *no doubt* that every Frog and every Toad was *once* a Tadpole, and swam in the water like a Fish and became a *Toad* which is what *all* tadpoles become, *unless of course,* they become Frogs, which is what happens to *Frog eggs,* with any luck, of course. At any rate, here is a story about a Frog and a Toad and some Tadpoles which, *of course,* will become Frogs and Toads.

Or the other way around, if you like . . . .

Now let's hear it from the Frog and the Toad! . . . .

or maybe vice versa . . . . RIBB-ET . . . . RIBB-ET.

Burrowing Tree Frog

Small Tree Frog

Panama Golden Frogs

Horned Frog

Poem

The Frog sat on the lily pad, with *large*
And *bulging eyes*,
And looked *all* around at the Flies and
The Fish looking oh *so wise*.

It never moved a muscle, with its hind
Legs ready to *spring*.
Though it flicked out its tongue as the
Flies flew by and the Birds began to sing.

Well along came a Toad going *hippity-hop*
And looked at her cousin the Frog.
And then with one jump it *flew* through
The air and landed on a *log*.

"You *know*," said the Toad to her cousin
The Frog, "I *seldom* go into the water."
And the Frog turned around and stared
At the Toad and said: "what makes you think
 you *oughta*?"

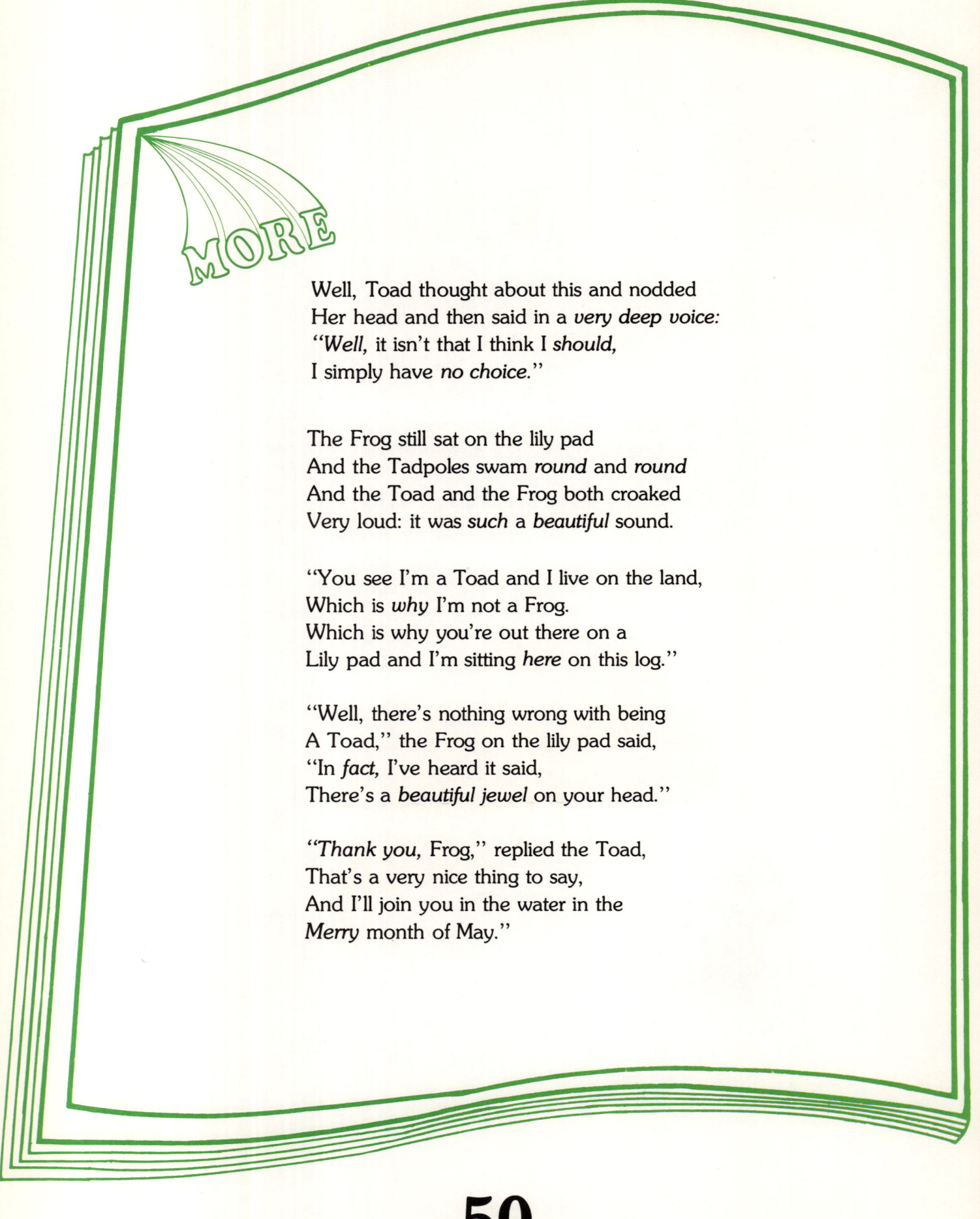

Well, Toad thought about this and nodded
Her head and then said in a *very deep voice:*
"Well, it isn't that I think I *should,*
I simply have *no choice."*

The Frog still sat on the lily pad
And the Tadpoles swam *round* and *round*
And the Toad and the Frog both croaked
Very loud: it was *such* a *beautiful* sound.

"You *see* I'm a Toad and I live on the land,
Which is *why* I'm not a Frog.
Which is why you're out there on a
Lily pad and I'm sitting *here* on this log."

"Well, there's nothing wrong with being
A Toad," the Frog on the lily pad said,
"In *fact,* I've heard it said,
There's a *beautiful jewel* on your head."

"Thank you, Frog," replied the Toad,
That's a very nice thing to say,
And I'll join you in the water in the
Merry month of May."

MORE

And having said this the Toad said
Goodbye with a *smile* and a *wink* of the eye.
And *jumped* off the log and disappeared
And the Frog caught another *fly*.

And *sure enough* in the month of May
The Toad returned to the water,
And laid *thousands of eggs* and
Watched them hatch; there were
Some *sons* and even a *daughter*.

The Frog still sat on the lily pad
And the tadpoles swam *round* and *round*
And the Toad and the Frog both croaked
Very loud: It was *such* a *beautiful* sound.

Now a Frog can be heard when it sings its song,
And Frogs have been known to croak,
And have you ever heard a Frog when it sings its song,
And wondered
What *language* it spoke?

There are Frogs that can jump and Toads that can hop
And they're such *fun* to have around.
And they fill the night in the countryside
With some really *fantastic* sound.

A *Bull,* of course, is *not* a Frog, and a Bullfrog *isn't a Bull.*
And you've *got* to admit that a Bull that's
A Frog is *really* adorable.

There are Frogs that live in the water,
And Toads that live on the land,
But you'll *never* see a Frog, or a Toad,
With its head buried in the *sand.*

Now a Tadpole's just a baby Frog or Toad
That looks just like a *Fish.*
But sooner or later a Tadpole's a Frog . . . or a Toad.
Is there more that a Tadpole could *wish?*

52

Now a Frog's not a Toad and a Toad's
Not a Frog, but they *certainly* look alike.

Though it's *well* to remember, and *never* forget,
That they *never* sing into a *mike*.

Now listen to a serenade to the Toad and to the Frog.
Then sing along and sing their song, ...
Or sing to the *Polywog!*

Frog Serenade

Sitting on a lily pad
In the sun,
Catching all the Flies
With your lightning tongue.

Lately I have heard that
My prince will come.
Tell me dear Frog
Are you the one?

RIBBET....RIBBET....RIBBET....RIBBET
A Frog serenade
Makes me think of summer days
And lemonade.

RIBB-ET....RIBB-ET....RIBB-ET....RIBB-ET
I hear you say
Maybe this might be *my*
Lucky day.

In your Tadpole days
You were so cute.
In your Froggy stage
You are a beaut!

Oh what a charming
Prince you'll be
With just one little kiss
From me.

Please don't hop away
You know today's your day.
Don't you know there's really nothing
Left to say?

If fairy tales
Are tried and true
One little kiss'll make
A Prince of you....*RIBB-ET....RIBB-ET*
RIBB-ET....RIBB-ET....RIBB-ET....RIBB-ET

The main function of the call of the Frog and the Toad is to bring the males and females together. Basically it is a mating call.

The males are the only ones that call. The females are attracted to this call and they home in on the male of their choice.

The call will attract a female only of the same species.

Sandra Keenan & Michael Kamen © Copyright 1977 ABC/Dunhill, Inc. Used by permission—all rights reserved.

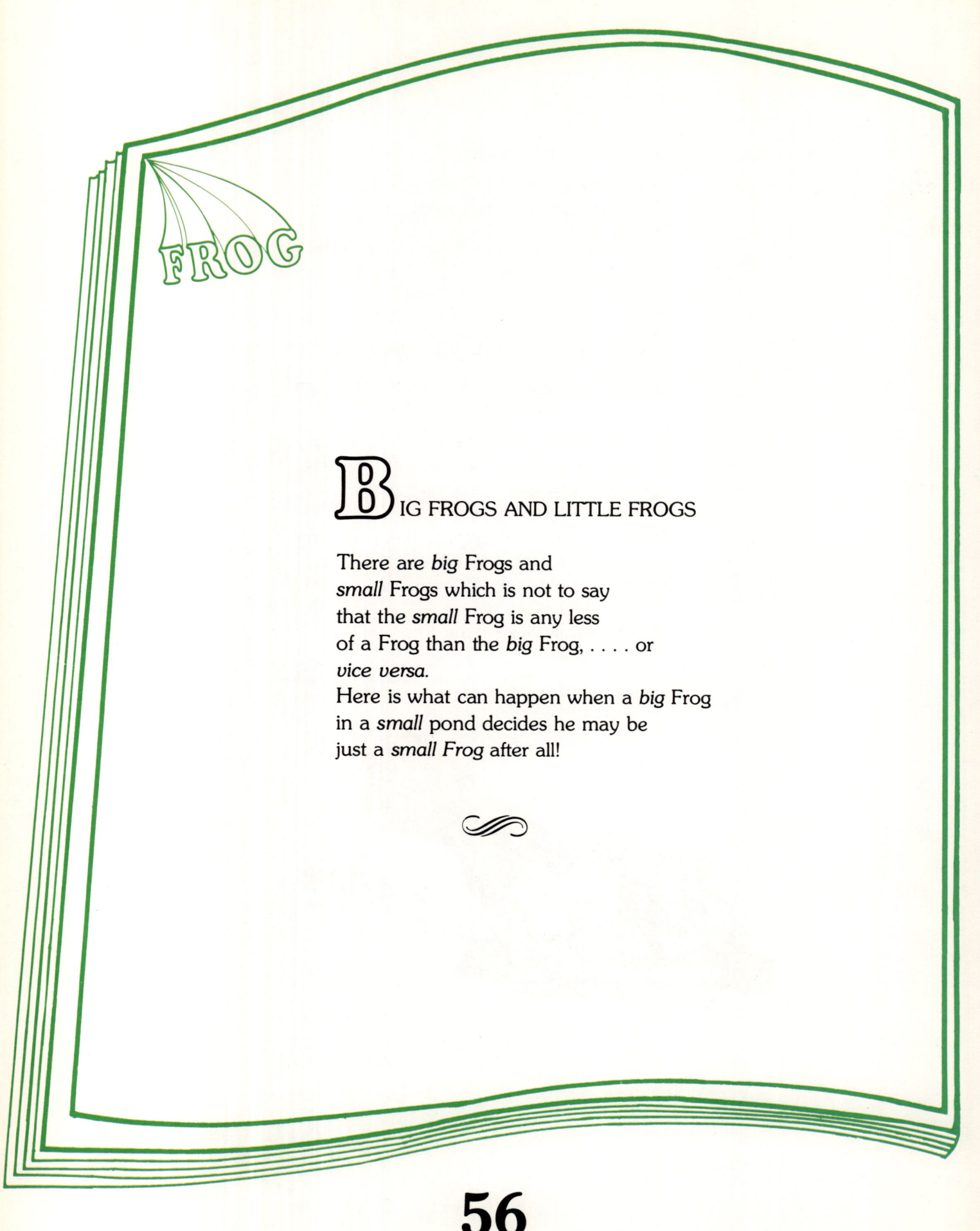

FROG

BIG FROGS AND LITTLE FROGS

There are *big* Frogs and
small Frogs which is not to say
that the *small* Frog is any less
of a Frog than the *big* Frog, ... or
vice versa.
Here is what can happen when a *big* Frog
in a *small* pond decides he may be
just a *small Frog* after all!

The Frog That Was Too Big for His Size

There once was a *very large Frog* in a *very small pond* which, of course, made this very large Frog feel *very* important, indeed, since as everyone knows, when you are a very large Frog in a very small pond you are *definitely* very much in charge.

Now as it happens, *as it usually happens in stories like this,* there were six other Frogs in this very small pond, and like the very large Frog, the six other Frogs were sunning themselves on six lily pads that were gently floating in the very small pond. Making *seven Frogs* sunning themselves on *seven lily pads* in the very small pond.

"I am," said the very large Frog in the very small pond, *"tired of being a very large Frog in a very small pond."*

Now the six other Frogs, who were sunning themselves on six lily pads floating gently in the very small pond, all turned to look at the very large Frog. They couldn't believe their ears, which, as everyone knows, are directly behind their eyes.

And one of them, the smallest of them all, *jumped* about two feet into the air, landing on another lily pad and said: "My friend, as you can see, I am a very small Frog in this very small pond..."

"**So**....?" said the very large Frog, sitting up with its long hind legs ready to jump.

"So," replied the very small Frog, "As a very small Frog in a very small pond, I have learned it isn't how big you are that matters, but how you play the game." And having said that, the very small Frog dove into the water leaving circles on circles, where she had disappeared.

Now the very large Frog in the very small pond thought about what the very small Frog had said. And at that very moment, as he scratched his head, a Dragonfly flew by. It circled once and then once more right over the very large Frog's head. It fluttered its wings and zoomed high and low and finally, landed right on the very large Frog's back.

"Hello, very large Frog," said the Dragonfly, still fluttering its wings. "Am I correct that I heard you say you're tired of being a very large Frog in a very small pond?"

"**Absolutely**," replied the very large Frog, turning his head with his bulging Frog eyes and the better to see the Dragonfly. "And I suppose, you would like to be a very large Frog in a very large pond?"

"Well, I did have something like that in mind," replied the very large Frog.

Now at this very moment, the other five Frogs that were sunning themselves on the lily pads in the very small pond, decided to jump into the water. And they did. And, of course, they disappeared like the very small Frog, leaving circles on circles.

This upset him *very* much since without the other six Frogs sunning themselves on the lily pads, there was no way to know whether he was a very *large* Frog in a very small pond, or a very *small* Frog in a very small pond.

So, turning to the Dragonfly once more, he said: "Dragonfly, I think I can be bigger than I am. **Watch**."

And so saying, the very large Frog, HUFFED and PUFFED and HUFFED some more, getting LARGER and **LARGER** and **LARGER.**

"*Frog,*" said the Dragonfly, "I *must* warn you, you'll *burst* if you continue to HUFF and PUFF and HUFF . . ."

But the very large Frog was determined to be BIGGER and BIGGER than any other Frog, even though there were no other Frogs left in the very small pond.

So he **HUFFED** some more and he **PUFFED** some more. And *sure* enough, he finally **EXPLODED!** leaving the Dragonfly fluttering its wings right where the very large Frog in the very small pond, sunning himself on a lily pad had been.

"*Poor Frog,* if only you had been satisfied to be what you were, which was a very large Frog in a very small pond, you would *still* be a Frog. What a pity!"

With which the Dragonfly flew off into the bright blue sky, and the six Frogs who had dived into the water suddenly *popped* their heads out, and *jumped* onto six lily pads and sunned themselves *once more* in the sun.

FROG

The Toad is not a Frog, and Vice Versa

A Toad is not a Frog and a Frog is not a Toad. The Toad, unlike the Frog, has short hind legs: the better to *hop* with. And while *Toads* are more often found in the garden and *Frogs* are more often found in ponds, a Frog, like a Toad, is an *Amphibian* or the other way around, ... if you like.

There is the game of *Leap Frog,* which is seldom played by Frogs, and people have been known to get a *Frog* in their throat, which certainly makes them almost *speechless,* in spite of the fact that a Frog in the throat is a figure of *speech.* Which brings us to the *Toad,* which we know, is not a *Frog,* though it is often mistaken for one, ... and vice versa.

And just in case anyone thinks a Frog is a Toad or a Toad is a Frog, or the other way around, after they see the following page, they will *definitely* know a Frog from a Toad and a Toad from a Frog, and, as I said, ... vice versa.

The Frog is of *course* a Frog
The Toad is of course a Toad.

THIS IS A FROG.

IT IS IN *FACT* A BULLFROG

THIS IS A TOAD.

IT IS A COLUMBIA GIANT TOAD

So as you can see, a Frog is not a Toad
and of course, ... vice versa.

As everyone knows-who-knows . . . . that a Frog is
a Frog, and a Toad is a Toad. Frogs, which are
not Toads, do not have *tails*. And Toads, which
are not Frogs, do not have tails. Which brings us
to the end of *this* tale about the Frog and the Toad,
though as *we* know, Frogs and Toads do not in any way,
have *tails*.

FROG

Now we know that a Frog-is-a-Frog,
and a Toad-is-a-Toad,

That Frogs jump and Toads hop,
that Frogs sing and Toads sing too,
and that there are some Frogs that are big
Frogs in a small pond, but might not be such
big Frogs in a big pond. Though of course a
big Frog in a small pond is no smaller when
he's in a big pond.

And that it isn't so bad to be a big Frog
in a small pond.

We might also remember that without the Frog
and the Toad to help us get rid of the Insects,
this would be a very itchy world indeed. Not that
I have anything against the Insects personally,
but I'm still glad the Toad and the Frog are around,
aren't *you*?

An animal is, of course, an animal, which is simply to say, there are Animals and there are animals, and if you add one more animal you have ANIMALS, ANIMALS, ANIMALS, which is the title of this book and all of the other books which, naturally enough, are titled ANIMALS, ANIMALS, ANIMALS. And so to all the animal lovers (and is there *anyone* who *isn't?*) we'll see you in the next edition of ANIMALS, ANIMALS, ANIMALS.

Bibliography

Pelicans

THE PELICANS
by George Laycock
The Natural History Press, Garden City, NY — 1970
58 pp.

WONDERS OF THE PELICAN WORLD
by Joseph J. Cook and Ralph W. Schreiber
Dodd, Mead & Company, NY — 1974
64 pp.

SCOOP, LAST OF THE BROWN PELICANS
by Robert M. McClung
William Morrow and Company, NY — 1972
64 pp.

THE BROWN PELICAN
by J. M. Roever
Steck-Vaughn Company, Austin, Texas — 1974
30 pp.

THE WONDERFUL PELICAN
by Jack Denton Scott
G. P. Putnam's Sons, NY — 1975
63 pp.

THE STORY OF MY PELICAN
by Albert Schweitzer
Hawthorn Books, Inc., NY — 1965
65 pp.

THE MIRACLE OF FLIGHT
by Richard Cromer
Doubleday & Company, Inc., Garden City, NY — 1968
159 pp.

WHAT MAKES A BIRD A BIRD?
by May Garelick
Follett Publishing Company, Chicago — 1969
32 pp.

Toads and Frogs

WONDERS OF FROGS AND TOADS
by Wyatt Blassingame
Dodd, Mead & Company, NY — 1975
80 pp.

FROGS AND TOADS OF THE WORLD
by Hilda Simon
J. B. Lippincott Company, Philadelphia — 1975
128 pp.

A FROG IS BORN
by William White, Jr.
Sterling Publishing Co., Inc., NY — 1972
80 pp.

THE FROG BOOK
Richard Shaw, Editor
Frederick Warne and Company, Inc., NY — 1972
48 pp.

FROGS AND TOADS
by Herbert S. Zim
William Morrow & Company, NY — 1950
57 pp.

A ZOO IN YOUR ROOM
by Roger Caras
Harcourt Brace Jovanovich, Inc., NY — 1975
96 pp.

THE FROG BOOK (Paperback)
by Mary C. Dickerson
Dover Publications, Inc., NY — 1969
253 pp.

Cats

DORIS BRYANT'S NEW CAT BOOK
by Doris Bryant
Ives Washburn, Inc., NY — 1969
181 pp.

CATNIP: SELECTING AND TRAINING YOUR CAT
by Kurt Unkelbach
Prentice-Hall, Inc., Englewood Cliffs, NJ — 1970
103 pp.

HOW KITTENS GROW
by Millicent E. Selsam
Four Winds Press, NY — 1973
32 pp.

THE LIFE, HISTORY AND MAGIC OF THE CAT
by Fernand Mery
Grosset & Dunlap, Inc., NY — 1968
235 pp.

KITTEN CABOODLE: A Selection of Feline Fiction
Barbara Silverberg, Editor
Holt, Rinehart and Winston, NY — 1969
204 pp.

WONDER TALES OF DOGS AND CATS
by Frances Carpenter
Doubleday & Company, Inc., Garden City, NY — 1955
255 pp.

THE CAT BOOK
Richard Shaw, Editor
Frederick Warne & Company, Inc., NY — 1973
48 pp.

BEST CAT STORIES
Michael Joseph, Editor
Robert Bentley, Inc., Boston, MA — 1953
271 pp.